025. 0637130 281

WEBSITES FOR

This boo
the

D0808570

Brookes

Developed in
association with

learn.co.uk

from *The***Guardian**

H O D D E R
Wayland

a division of Hodder Headline Limited

Text copyright © Learnthings Ltd and Kate Brookes 2002
Illustrations © Learnthings Ltd
Cover design Stewart Larking
Design by Fiona Webb

First published in Great Britain in 2002 by Hodder Wayland,
an imprint of Hodder Children's Books.
This edition published in 2003.

10 9 8 7 6 5 4 3 2 1

A catalogue record for this book is available from the
British Library.

ISBN: 0 7502 44682

Hodder Children's Books
a division of Hodder Headline Limited
338 Euston Road
London NW1 3BH

Printed and bound in Great Britain

CONTENTS

INTRODUCTION

Whether you're trying to solve a maths problem, research coursework assignments or looking for D&T project ideas, you'll find it on the Internet!

But with so much stuff on the web – some good, some bad – finding exactly what you need can mean hours glued to a screen. Even then, there's no guarantee of hitting the best and most relevant site. That is, until now!

Top Websites for Homework takes you straight to the best websites for National Curriculum subjects from KS2 to KS4 and beyond to AS subjects. You'll find answers, online lessons, homework help, background information, primary sources, texts, and inspiration for everything from Roald Dahl to Martin Luther King.

All the sites mentioned here are recommended by **learn.co.uk** – *The Guardian* newspaper's online resource for the National Curriculum – and are the 'pick' of **Six of the best** and the **Web guide**. Each entry includes the hyperlink location and URL address along with a brief description of the site and the key stage. In addition, sites are ranked in order of 'difficulty'. Sites that are easy to navigate and present basic but essential information in the simplest way are listed first.

Only a small proportion of the thousands of sites on **learn.co.uk** could be mentioned in this book. In addition to the subjects covered here – English, maths, science, history, geography, design and technology, arts, modern languages, citizenship, PSHE and RE – **Six of the best** and the **Web guide** also cover: business studies, careers, classics, economics, law, literacy, media studies, physical education, philosophy and ethics, politics, separate sciences and Welsh.

All sites have been rigorously checked for suitability. However, links often change but are updated regularly. Visit **learn.co.uk** for URL updates.

The following is a list of **learn.co.uk's** educational experts and advisers who trawled the Internet day and night to find the best homework, revision and research sites for you. This book contains only a small fraction of their hard work. Go to **learn.co.uk** for the best of the rest.

Primary Les Snowdon and Maggie Humphreys
KS3 English John Mannion
KS4 Maths Linda Amrane-Cooper
KS4 Science Nick Falk
KS3 Geography Mark Ellis
KS3 History John Simkin
KS3 Design and Technology Andy Davies
KS4 French Anneli McLachlan
KS3 Citizenship Larry Hartley

Thanks also to **EducationGuardian.co.uk** for their initial research on the **Web guide**, and to Jim Merrett and Lyndsey Turner, who contributed to Education Guardian's weekly column, **On the web**.

ENGLISH

This chapter takes you from KS2 Literacy via fiction, poetry and plays to writing.

If the sites described here don't cover the right aspect or topic, then cruise the **Web guide** at **learn.co.uk.** Once the English menu pops up, simply click on the topic for direct access to the site. You will find hundreds of sites on the following English topics: Shakespeare, the Brontë sisters, HG Wells, Jonathan Swift, Robert Louis Stevenson, DH Lawrence, Thomas Hardy, William Golding, Charles Dickens, Daniel Defoe, Sir Arthur Conan Doyle, Jane Austen, James Joyce and George Eliot. There are also more general websites for poetry, language and drama.

For online English KS2 to KS4 and AS-level lessons, go to:
learn.co.uk > Online lessons and tests

FICTION

Go to: learn.co.uk ▶ Web guide ▶ Primary

➲ The Big Myth

Twenty-seven world creation myth stories from Aztec to Zulu. Great graphics and sound effects. Not just for KS2, but for everyone.

http://www.bigmyth.com/

➲ Roald Dahl

Discover more about Roald Dahl the man, and his stories. Flash 4 or 5 plug-ins are needed to view this site. Best for KS2.

http://www.roalddahl.com/

Go to: learn.co.uk ▶ Guardian resources ▶ Primary ▶ On the web ▶ Poetry

➲ Jabberwocky

A great place to read up on Lewis Carroll, creator of *Alice in Wonderland*, and his novels and poetry.

http://www.jabberwocky.com/carroll/jabber/ jabberwocky.html

⊃ Ted Dewan and Helen Cooper

This is one of the best author sites around.
Dewan and Cooper, husband and wife illustrators
and authors of children's books, give KS2 a tour of
how ideas become books.

http://www.wormworks.com/

⊃ Paul Jennings

If you're a fan of the 'Gizmo' books, this is a
chance to find out what makes the author tick.
Suitable for KS2-3.

http://www.pauljennings.com.au/index.htm

⊃ Harry Potter Fan Site

Harry and his author JK Rowling are
bound to become the subjects
of homework projects. If there's
anything you don't know, then
head to the Harry Potter Times.

http://www.geocities.com/thepottersite/

HOW TO READ A NOVEL

Go to: learn.co.uk ▶ Web guide ▶ English
▶ The Brontë Sisters

➲ Charlotte Brontë Essays

Go to: learn.co.uk ▶ Online lessons and tests ▶
KS4 English literature - Prose ▶ 20th Century

➲ The Lord of the Flies

These two sites are not just excellent sources
of information on the Brontë sisters
and William Golding's *The Lord of
the Flies*, they also teach you how to
read a novel so that you can analyse
everything from plot, character and
genre to the setting, theme and
language. KS3 and KS4 will find both
sites worth a visit.

WILLIAM GOLDING

Go to: learn.co.uk ▶ Six of the best ▶ English
▶ KS4 William Golding's Lord of the Flies

⮑ Biography of William Golding

A biography along with personal
thoughts from Golding himself.
http://www.kirjasto.sci.fi/wgolding.htm

⮑ Plot, characters, themes, symbolism and a map

If pictures help you learn, then you won't want
to miss this 3-D version of the island in *Lord of
the Flies*, and snaps from the original film. There's
also explanations of Golding's symbolism and
summaries of each chapter.
http://www.gerenser.com/lotf/

⮑ Study guide

One click and you've come to the serious 'Flies'
site. Overlook it at your peril!
http://www.learn.co.uk/default.asp?
WCI=Unit&WCU=2615

GEORGE ORWELL

Go to: learn.co.uk ▶ Six of the best
▶ English ▶ KS4 George Orwell's Animal Farm

⊃ Orwell biography

A concise biography followed by thoughts from Orwell on why he wrote.

http://www.spartacus.schoolnet.co.uk/Jorwell.htm

⊃ Essays and background on George Orwell

"*What I have most wanted to do during the past ten years is to turn political writing into an art.*" (Orwell, 1946) This quote and others make a visit to the site well worthwhile.

http://www.seas.upenn.edu/~allport/chestnut/

⊃ Plot summary and explanation of the symbolism

Don't be put off by the amount of text on this site as it is all valuable.

http://www.k-1.com/Orwell/animf.htm

CHARLES DICKENS

Go to: learn.co.uk ▶ Six of the best ▶ English
▶ KS3 Charles Dickens

⊃ The Victorian web

Start here. The home page says it all – genre and
mode, literary relations, characterisation, imagery,
narrative, themes, biography, and list of works.
http://65.107.211.206/dickens/dickensov.html

⊃ Dickens' London

A snapshot of London in 1865 which
is invaluable for understanding
Dickens. Head to the photo archives
for KS3 and KS4 history.
http://humwww.ucsc.edu/dickens/
OMF/1865.html

⊃ Discovering Dickens

This site provides the tools for you to create a
Dickens timeline, diary, storyboard or poster.
http://www.west.net/~cybrary/Dickens/

⊃ Dickens page

Ask the Dickens expert a question and get an answer! Also good to look at when studying Dickensian London and Dickens in America.
http://www.fidnet.com/~dap1955/dickens/index.html

Go to: learn.co.uk ▶ Guardian resources
▶ Secondary ▶ On the web ▶ The Victorian novel

⊃ Novel Guide

This site analyses over 70 novels and dramas. It goes beyond the Victorian novel and takes in Shakespeare, Aldous Huxley, Plato, Alice Walker, F. Scott Fitzgerald and more. Valuable for KS3-4.
http://www.novelguide.com

⊃ A Brief List of Some Key Terms in Literature

A-Z of definitions of literary terms, along with examples and links. Best for KS3-4 and beyond.
http://courses.nus.edu.sg/course/ellibst/lsl01-tm.html

REFERENCE

Go to: learn.co.uk ▶ Web guide ▶ English

➲ **Achuka – Children's Books UK**
Interviews with all your favourite authors.
http://www.achuka.co.uk

➲ **Author Webliography**
Thousands of links to literary greats.
http://www.lib.lsu.edu/hum/authors.html

➲ **Bibliomania.com**
The text of 2000 books along with study guides,
dictionaries and biographies.
http://www.bibliomania.com/

➲ **Books Unlimited**
This Guardian newspaper site covers
poetry and literature – much of it
very contemporary. For biographies,
go to 'Author'.
http://books.guardian.co.uk

POETRY

Go to: learn.co.uk ▶ Guardian resources
▶ Primary ▶ On the web ▶ Poetry

➲ Poetry for kids

Funny poems and how to write them by Kenn
Nesbitt for KS2.

http://poetry4kids.com/

Go to: learn.co.uk ▶ Web guide
▶ English ▶ Poetry

➲ Caribbean Poets

A hot site for Caribbean poetry and literature.

http://www.freenet.hamilton.on.ca/~aa462/
cariblit.html/

➲ Atlantic Monthly Poetry Pages

A world poetry feast for KS4 and beyond. Real
Audio required to listen to the poetry sound files.

http://www.theatlantic.com/unbound/poetry/
poetpage.htm

Go to: learn.co.uk ▶ Guardian resources
▶ Secondary ▶ On the web ▶ Online poetry

➲ Poet's Corner

Some 6,700 works by 780 poets that are located
by clicking on the A-Z by name or title.
http://www.geocities.com/~spanoudi/poems/
index.html

➲ Bartleby

Huge verse and literature resource. Your teachers
may be familiar with it, so ask their advice about
where to look for relevant material. Best for
KS3-4 and above.
http://www.bartleby.com

Go to: learn.co.uk ▶ Guardian resources
▶ Primary ▶ On the web ▶ Poetry

➲ Haiku

Discover what Haiku is all about, how to do it,
and some great examples.
http://www.toyomasu.com/haiku

Go to: learn.co.uk ▶ Web guide ▶ English
▶ Poetry

⊃ The Great War

Poetry of WWI is a large part of this history site
and includes the work of Wilfred Owen, Siegfreid
Sassoon, Robert Graves and others. Hit
'Bloomsbury Magazine' for a study course.
http://www.pitt.edu/~pugachev/greatwar/ww1.html

TED HUGHES

Go to: learn.co.uk ▶ Six of the best
▶ KS4 English ▶ Ted Hughes

⊃ Biography, articles and links

A very wordy site with lots of insight and links
worth exploring.
http://www.uni-leipzig.de/~angl/hughes.index2.htm

⊃ Ted Hughes' home page

Thirteen essays on Hughes' work, life and death.
http://www.zeta.org.au/~annskea/THHome.htm

PLAYS

WILLIAM SHAKESPEARE

Go to: learn.co.uk ▶ Six of the best ▶ English
▶ KS3 William Shakespeare

➲ The Globe Theatre

There's the archaeology of the Globe, 16th-17th
century London Playhouses and timeline. Useful
for KS3-4 English, history and drama.
http://www.rdg.ac.uk/globe/

➲ Surfing with the Bard

Everything from comedies to poetry. A discussion
zone and frequently asked questions. Don't miss
the 'fun zone' where Shakespeare meets a Trekkie.
http://www.ulen.com/shakespeare/

➲ The Shakespeare Birthplace Trust

Study material on *Othello* and *The Tempest* for
upper KS3 and KS4.
http://www.shakespeare.org.uk/

➲ Chill with Will

Romeo and Juliet, Julius Caesar, Hamlet and *Macbeth* essays and guides. Audio quotes are available to download.

http://library.thinkquest.org/19539/front.htm

➲ Shakespeare online

A comprehensive site with essays on themes like friendship. Check out 'What the Bard Didn't Say' and the Elizabethan glossary.

http://www.shakespeare-online.com/

Go to: learn.co.uk ▶ Web guide ▶ English ▶ Shakespeare

➲ The Shakespeare Insulter

Learn Elizabethan English insults to impress your friends. Here's one to get you going:
"Were I like thee I'd throw away myself"
(*Timon of Athens*)

http://www.pangloss.com/seidel/Shaker/

ARTHUR MILLER

Go to: learn.co.uk ▶ Six of the best
▶ English KS4 Arthur Miller's The Crucible

Read the scheme of work for a reminder of what
will get you marks – themes, characterisations,
plot, imagery, social and historical context, etc.

➲ Salem trials home page
The history of the events in Salem in 1692 and
information about 'The Crucible'.
http://www.law.umkc.edu/faculty/projects/ftrials/salem
/salem.htm

Go to: learn.co.uk ▶ Guardian resources
▶ Secondary ▶ On the web ▶ Arthur Miller

➲ Arthur Miller Teaching Resources
Best for KS4 and above, this site covers Miller's
'All my Sons', 'The Crucible' and 'Death of a
Salesman'.
http://www.webenglishteacher.com/miller.html

WRITING

Go to: learn.co.uk ▶ Guardian resources
▶ Primary ▶ On the web ▶ Creative writing

➲ The writing process
Clear look at the ABC's of writing – prewriting, writing, editing, revising, etc.
http://www.angelfire.com/wi/writingprocess/prewriting.html

GRAMMAR, SPELLING AND PUNCTUATION

Go to: learn.co.uk ▶ Web guide ▶ Literacy

➲ Wacky Web Tales
Good fill-in-the-missing word activities for KS2.
http://www.eduplace.com/tales

➲ Six hundred words ...
If you can't spell 'accommodation', 'miscellaneous' or 'weird', and don't know your 'our' from your 'are' then download this document.

> Go to: learn.co.uk ▶ Online lessons and
> tests ▶ KS3 English language

This Learn material covers punctuation, spelling,
sentences and attainments in reading and listening.
http://www.learn.co.uk/default.asp?WCI=Topic&WC
U=3946

> Go to: learn.co.uk ▶ Six of the best
> ▶ English ▶ KS4 Grammar

➲ Frequently asked grammar questions

Go straight to the 'Articles' window for sound
grammar help.
http://www.protrainco.com/grammar.htm

➲ Grammar quizzes

Go straight to 'Quizzes' and start at the top.
http://www.brownlee.org/durk/grammar

➲ Basic grammar and style

The 'Anatomy of a Sentence' pulls a sentence to
pieces and labels each part.
http://www.shared-visions.com/explore/english/

WRITING TO PERSUADE

Go to: learn.co.uk ▶ Six of the best
▶ English ▶ KS4 Charity

Read the Scheme of Work for a quick reminder
of what persuasive writing is and what's required
for an effective piece of homework. Targeted for
KS4, but fine for KS3. To back up your assignment
with real-world examples, here are five charity
sites which employ persuasive writing:

➲ WWF

The Living Planet Campaign site
is clear about its aims and its
target audience: "... *to encourage
individuals, corporations and
governments to take action.*"
A good example of how to
target your writing.
http://www.panda.org/livingplanet/

➲ Shelter
Great press releases to guide public opinion (via the media) to an understanding that the *"situation facing young homeless people is nothing short of a scandal"*. Worth a visit.
http://www.shelter.org.uk/

➲ RSPCA
Compare this site with one of the others to see how presentation and tone vary according to the target audience.
http://www.rspca.org.uk/

➲ NSPCC
Unlike the other sites, this one has a single focus – the FULL STOP Campaign. Go to the Kids' Zone and consider the value of celebrity endorsements.
http://www.nspcc.org.uk/homepage/

➲ Oxfam Horn of Africa appeal
News releases, reports and photographs on Oxfam's work in drought-devastated Ethiopia.
http://www.oxfam.org.uk/atwork/emerg/ethiopia.htm

MATHS

When it comes to maths homework, you want explanations and answers pronto, and that is what the **learn.co.uk** online lesson sites do (see pages 30-34). They will walk you through the topic, checking along the way that you are keeping up to speed and give you lots of examples. The **learn.co.uk** lesson sites cover the curriculum from KS2 to KS4 at all levels and tiers.

On pages 35-49, there's more homework help on a range of topics from the basics of mental maths through to simultaneous equations and trigonometry. If you're checking out a topic for the first time or trying to understand it in more detail, then start with the first recommended site.

KS2 MATHS

Can't do your homework because you missed a lesson or weren't actually concentrating in class? Don't worry, **learn.co.uk** will take you over the whole thing.

> Go to: learn.co.uk ▶ Online lessons and tests

⊃ **KS2 Mathematics**
Click on the topic (e.g. Numbers, Handling Data or Shape, Space and Measurement) and then click on the specific item that's giving you homework grief (e.g. mean, median, mode, or range).

KS3 MATHS

The whole maths curriculum is here, so if you've hit a homework snag, head to the following and get it sorted!

Go to: learn.co.uk ▶ Online lessons and tests
▶ KS3 Mathematics

➲ Number

Number system, negative numbers, indices, roots, decimals, fractions, percentages, ratio, proportion, estimation, mental maths, and using a calculator.

➲ Algebra

Sequences and patterns, algebraic expressions, linear equations, inequalities, graphs, simultaneous equations, and formulae.

➲ Shape, space and measurement

Lines and angles, triangles, quadrilaterals, transformations and symmetry, circle, solids, polygons, transformation geometry, measures, transformations and co-ordinates, construction, and loci.

➲ Handling data

Collecting, presenting and interpreting data, and probability.

KS4 MATHS FOUNDATION

Go to: learn.co.uk ▶ Online lessons and tests
▶ KS4 Mathematics – Foundation

⊃ Number and algebra

Place value and decimals, types of numbers, working with fractions and negative numbers, ratio and proportion, using variables, linear equations, trial and improvement, formulae, number sequences, interpreting graphs, and more.

⊃ Shape, space and measurement

Angles and triangles, congruency and similarity, quadrilaterals, perimeter, area and volume, symmetry and polygons, circles, scales and bearings, transformations, units and measure, and 3-D figures.

⊃ Handling data

Collecting, processing and interpreting data, presenting data, averages, and probability.

KS4 MATHS HIGHER

Go to: learn.co.uk ▶ Online lessons and tests
▶ KS4 Mathematics – Higher

➲ Number and algebra

Using and applying mathematics, understanding the basics of numbers, fractions and decimals, using basic number skills, equations and inequalities, lines, simultaneous equations and regions, using brackets in algebra, estimation and approximation, sequences and formulae, using proportion and proportionality, working with graphs, simplifying algebraic expressions, quadratic equations, irrational numbers, application of transformations, rates of change and areas under graphs, modelling to understand relationships, and calculators and computers.

⊃ Shape, space and measures

Recognising shapes, transformations, loci,
Pythagoras' theorem, trigonometry (introduction),
advanced trigonometry, perimeter, area and
volume, advanced perimeter, area and volume,
vectors, and circle geometry.

⊃ Handling data

Collecting data, presenting data, correlation and
scatter diagrams, measures of central tendency,
measures of spread, interpretation of graphs, and
probability.

CORE STUFF

Maths is a subject that is repetitive in nature. For example, the topic of probability first appears at KS2 but re-appears at KS4 and beyond. That's why it's so important to have a firm grasp of the essentials so that as the topic gets 'harder' you stay on top!

Go to: learn.co.uk ▶ Web guide
▶ Numeracy

➲ Megamaths
Concentrating on multiplication tables and shapes, this BBC site drills home KS2 essentials.
http://www.bbc.co.uk/education/megamaths/

➲ Ambleside Primary School Numeracy Activities
Much of the material is for a KS2 teacher, but there's lots of homework help as well.
http://www.ambleside.schoolzone.co.uk/ambleweb/numeracy.htm

➲ BasketMath Interactive Learning

Every time you get a correct answer, the basketball player slam dunks a ball into the hoop. Work your way through the questions from top to bottom.

http://www.scienceacademy.com/BI/

Go to: learn.co.uk ▶ Six of the best
▶ Maths ▶ KS2 Maths – Decimals

➲ Interactive fraction-to-decimal game

Change the numerator and denominator, click the 'Decifractator' machine and bingo! up comes the decimal equivalent.

http://www.ambleside.schoolzone.co.uk/ambleweb/mentalmaths/fracto.html

Go to: learn.co.uk ▶ Six of the best ▶ Maths
▶ KS2 Maths – Multiplication and Division

➲ Division and multiplication

No matter what key stage, you'll find down to earth help here.

http://www.learn.co.uk/default.asp?WCI=Topic&WCU=6966

Go to: learn.co.uk ▶ Six of the best
▶ Maths ▶ KS2 Maths – Symmetry

➲ Shapes investigation and reflection

Go right back to basics and learn shapes –
rectangles through to regular decagons – and
their properties.
http://www.bbc.co.uk/education/megashapes/invest/
text01.shtml

Go to: learn.co.uk ▶ Web guide ▶ Mathematics

➲ Maths Lessons that are fun, fun, fun!

Fun might be pushing it, but the lessons on
fractions, geometry and algebra are highly
recommended.
http://math.rice.edu/~lanius/Lessons/

➲ Compvter Romanvs

If you've ever puzzled over
Roman numerals, you'll find the
answer on this slightly wacky site.
http://www.naturalmath.
com/tool2.html

➲ Maths Goodies
Choose a KS3 topic – statistics, percent, area, circumference, number theory – then dive in!
http://www.mathgoodies.com/

Go to: learn.co.uk ▶ Web guide
▶ Mathematics ▶ Problem solving

➲ Word Problems For Kids
From the dead-easy to the dead-hard, these problems will help you suss-out the simple maths in word problems.
http://www.stfx.ca/special/mathproblems/welcome.html

Go to: learn.co.uk ▶ Web guide
▶ Mathematics ▶ Numbers & money

➲ Fractions, Decimals, Percentages
Head here if you're less than wonderful at converting fractions and the rest.
http://mathforum.org/dr.math/faq/faq.fractions.html

➲ BEATCALC: Beat the Calculator!

Put away your calculator and put on your thinking cap for some mind-exhausting mental maths tests.
http://mathforum.org/k12/mathtips/beatcalc.html

Go to: learn.co.uk ▸ Six of the best
▸ Maths ▸ KS2 Mass

➲ Problems involving weighing

Worksheets on lots of topics, including weighing, that you can print out and fill in. Good for KS1-2.
http://www.primaryresources.co.uk/maths/
maths7.htm

Go to: learn.co.uk ▸ Web guide ▸
Mathematics ▸ Data management

➲ Data Analysis

Key 'problem solver' into search box and click on Webmath. On problem solver page, click on your topic for explanations and answers.
http://school.discovery.com/homeworkhelp/webmath

Go to: learn.co.uk ▶ Web guide
▶ Mathematics ▶ KS2 Games and puzzles

➲ **The Grey Labyrinth**

Puzzles of varying difficulty to solve when you've finished homework!

http://www.greylabyrinth.com/index.htm

GRAPHING

Go to: learn.co.uk ▶ Six of the best
▶ Maths ▶ KS4 Graphing

➲ **Help with graphing straight lines**

Start here to learn about plotting co-ordinates and solving equations.

http://www.accessone.com/%7Ebbunge/Algebra/
Algebra.html

➲ **Online graphing: 2D and 3D**

Key in your KS3 (or above) algebra problem and one of the calculators will solve it.

http://www.algebrahelp.com/calculators/

EQUATIONS

Go to: learn.co.uk ▶ Web guide
▶ Mathematics ▶ Algebra

➲ Solving Equations
Click on a problem solver, key in your equation
and the answer and an explanation will appear.
http://school.discovery.com/homeworkhelp/
webmath/

Go to: learn.co.uk ▶ Six of the best
▶ Maths ▶ KS4 Solving equations

➲ Step-by-step help with solving equations
Decide what problem you need solved, and then
click to reveal a solution.
http://www.edteach.com/algebra/table_of_contents.
htm

➲ Online help with algebra
Go here if you haven't got the technology to
access the previous site.
http://www.algebrahelp.com

Go to: learn.co.uk ▶ Six of the best ▶ Maths
▶ KS4 Simultaneous equations and inequalities

⊃ How to solve simultaneous equations

Independent, dependent and inconsistent
equations simply explained.

http://www.edteach.com/algebra/systems/solution_
set.htm

⊃ Challenging problems with answers

Equations homework tragedy? Head here for help
and explanations.

http://nrich.maths.org/topic_tree/Algebra/Equations/
Simultaneous_Linear/index.html

⊃ Word problems involving two variables, with help

Let Dr Math show you how to
solve word problems with up to
five variables.

http://mathforum.com/dr.math/
faq/faq.age.problems.html

PROBABILITY

Go to: learn.co.uk ▶ Six of the best
▶ Maths ▶ KS4 Probability

➲ More help with probability

More of a revision site for KS4, but bound to
solve any homework hassles.
http://www.bbc.co.uk/education/gcsebitesize/maths/
data_handling_foundation_intermediate/probability_
rev.shtml

➲ Probability and the Lottery

You have a 1 in 14 million chance of winning the
Lottery. See how this is worked out.
http://www.maths-help.co.uk/Knowldge/Stat/Lottery/
Question.htm

DATA HANDLING

Go to: learn.co.uk ▶ Six of the best ▶ Maths
▶ KS4 Data handling

➲ Help with aspects of data handling

Intended for KS4 Higher with histograms,
probability and sampling, but information is so
clearly presented that it will help KS4 foundation
and KS3.

http://www.bbc.co.uk/education/gcsebitesize/maths/
data_handling_higher/index.shtml

➲ Help with standard deviation

That's the only thing this site
does, but it does it so well!
Before long you'll be a master of
standard deviation.

http://www.gcseguide.co.uk/
standard_deviation.htm

TRIGONOMETRY

Go to: learn.co.uk ▶ Web guide
▶ Mathematics ▶ Trigonometry

➲ Dave's Short Trig Course

Dave delivers the goods on trigonometry to bring you up to speed.

http://aleph0.clarku.edu/~djoyce/java/trig/

Go to: learn.co.uk ▶ Six of the best
▶ Maths ▶ KS4 Trigonometry

➲ Graphing of trigonometric functions

Start here if you feel that "trigonometry is a big, ugly, hairy monster that will make you green, scream and die!"

http://catcode.com/trig/index.html

➲ Cool links, including vectors and music

This SOS trigonometry site is a gem for KS4.

http://www.coolmath.com/links_trig.htm

FRACTALS

Go to: learn.co.uk ▶ Six of the best
▶ Maths ▶ KS4 Fractals

➲ **Learn more about fractals while making your own**

A really good introduction to your first lessons in fractals.

http://math.rice.edu/~lanius/frac/

➲ **What is a fractal?**

Have some fun clicking on the fractal image, changing its colours and observing what happens as you look at smaller sections.

http://mathforum.org/alejandre/applet.mandlebrot.html

➲ **Images of fractals**

Never before has maths been so beautiful! Click on the fractals to discover why.

http://www.iconbazaar.com/fractals/index.html

PYTHAGORAS' THEOREM

Go to: learn.co.uk ▶ Six of the best
▶ Maths ▶ KS4 Pythagoras' theorem

➲ Visit Pythagoras' playground to discover your way around the world

Do quadrant projects, measure the time with your hands and jolly-around with $a^2+b^2=c^2$.

http://www.kyes-world.com/pythagor.htm

➲ Pythagoras' theorem

A quick do-it-yourself demo of Pythagoras' theory that will take just two minutes. Do it!

http://www.ies.co.jp/math/products/geo2/applets/pytha2/pytha2.html

➲ History of Pythagoras

If you want to know about the man and his times, this is the place. Easy on the eye, and on the brain!

http://www.bbc.co.uk/education/archive/local_heroes97/biogpythagoras.shtml

FIBONACCI NUMBERS AND THE GOLDEN RATIO

Go to: learn.co.uk ▶ Six of the best ▶ Maths
▶ KS4 Fibonacci Numbers and the
Golden Ratio

⮑ **Fibonacci numbers and nature**
Fibonacci's rabbits, shell spirals, seed heads, pine cones and much more.
http://www.mcs.surrey.ac.uk/Personal/R.Knott/Fibonacci/fibnat.html

⮑ **Some Fibonacci puzzles**
These are described as 'easier'
puzzles, but thankfully answers
and explanations are provided.
http://www.mcs.surrey.ac.uk/
Personal/R.Knott/Fibonacci/
fibpuzzles.html

PASCAL'S TRIANGLE

Go to: learn.co.uk ▶ Six of the best
▶ Maths ▶ KS4 Pascal's triangle

➲ Explore pizza and hidden cubes through Pascal's triangle

Go here if you are just starting this topic.

http://mathforum.com/workshops/usi/pascal/pascal_lessons.html#lessons

➲ Patterns and colours in Pascal's triangle

Feed in the divisor of your choice and watch Pascal's triangle transform.

http://www.cs.washington.edu/homes/jbaer/classes/blaise/blaise.html

➲ Amazing Pascal's triangle facts

All you ever need to know about Pascal's triangle, but were afraid you might be told.

http://myhome.hananet.net/~daiyongk/mathtest/pascalnote2.files/ptri2.htm

SCIENCE

Your first stop for science homework help should be **learn.co.uk** > **Online lessons and tests** where you will find the complete curriculum for KS2-KS4 and AS science at all levels and tiers.

For science projects, here are two excellent sites that each cover vast scientific territory:

> Go to: learn.co.uk ▶ Six of the best ▶ Science ▶ KS4 Food chains

➲ **Movie and quiz to help students understand the relationship between webs and chains**

http://www.brainpop.com/science/ecology/foodchains/index.weml

> Go to: learn.co.uk ▶ Six of the Best ▶ Science ▶ Acids and alkalis

➲ **Acid base neutralisation, with animation**

http://www.sprocketworks.com/shockwave/load.asp?SprMovie=chemacidsbasesweb

LIFE PROCESSES AND LIVING THINGS

Go to: learn.co.uk ▶ Six of the best
▶ Science ▶ KS4 Food chains

➲ Choose a habitat and find out who eats what

Click on 'Habitat' to discover what lives there and how it survives. Good for KS2.

http://www.naturegrid.org.uk/

➲ Turn your class into a food chain

An outdoor Survival Game to organise with friends that demonstrates the food chain and its intricate workings.

http://collections.ic.gc.ca/science/english/bio/projects/foodchan.html

⊃ The flow of energy in a simple food chain

Fine for KS3 and KS4 as it gradually builds up into a detailed study of food chains and systems with a sound glossary and good links.

http://www.geog.ouc.bc.ca/physgeog/contents/4e.html

Go to: learn.co.uk ▶ Six of the best ▶ Primary ▶ The human body and health

⊃ Human anatomy

Click on the system you want to know more about – respiratory, digestive, excretory, etc.– and then move the cursor over the image for additional facts. Good for KS2-3.

http://www.innerbody.com/htm/body.html

⊃ Human reproduction

Short, easy-to-read text for KS2 homework/projects and KS3 short answer questions. Click to explore other systems.

http://tqjunior.thinkquest.org/5250/Reproduc.htm

⊃ Staying healthy

Look here for anything to do with health and
nutrition for KS2-3 science, food technology,
design and technology and PSHE. Food pyramid
material is excellent.
http://www.kidshealth.org/kid/stay_healthy

⊃ Food and health

A vast site that will be helpful for KS3-4 science,
food technology, design and technology (KS2-3
only) and PSHE. Every aspect of nutrition and
food safety is covered, with an excellent reference
to food commodities.
http://www.nutrition.org.uk

⊃ Online exploration of the heart

Go straight to the contents page for a particular
topic, or enjoy the 'Preview Gallery' with its
open-heart surgery movie among other
multimedia delights. Sound reference for KS3-4.
http://sln.fi.edu/biosci/heart.html

LIVING THINGS AND THEIR ENVIRONMENT

Go to: learn.co.uk ▶ Six of the best
▶ Primary ▶ The environment

➲ Minibeasts

Click on the trivia for some amazing facts about
minibeasts. The pictures aren't great, but the text
is just right for KS2-3 projects.

http://www.members.aol.com/YESedu/minimenu.html

➲ The weather

Go to the pull-down menu or click on the sun
icon to follow set paths through entire themes.
Definitive site for KS2-3.

http://www.cloudsrus.com

➲ Water science

Everything you could ever want to know about
water for science and geography projects. Dip
your toe in the H_2O for water basics.

http://wwwga.usgs.gov/edu/mearthgw.html

Go to: learn.co.uk ▶ Web guide
▶ Biology

⊃ Insect bios

Close-up photography on a limited range of
creepy-crawlies, supported with simple facts
about the creatures. Don't miss the butterfly
wing patterns.

http://www.insects.org/

⊃ Yucky.com

Described as the yuckiest site
on the web! It covers the less-
savoury facts about worms,
roaches, insects and the human
body. Not for the squeamish!

http://yucky.kids.discovery.com

⊃ Biology4Kids

Straightforward text on cell biology, ecology,
biochemistry, scientific enquiry and classification
for KS3-4.

http://www.biology4kids.com/index.html

Go to: learn.co.uk ▶ Six of the best ▶ Science
▶ KS4 Global warming

➲ Global warming

A government site that is geared towards 7-11
year-olds and 12-16 year-olds.
http://www.defra.gov.uk/environment/climatechange/
schools/index.htm

➲ Earth on fire

Discover the causes of global warming in the
Rogue's Gallery. Then check out solutions in this
site for KS2-4.
http://www.cotf.edu/ete/modules/carbon/earthfire.
html

➲ Understanding the forecast

A really interesting, interactive picture of global
warming. All levels welcome.
http://www.edf.org/pubs/Brochures/GlobalWarming/

➲ About global warming

Articles from the *New Scientist* magazine, for KS3-4.
http://www.newscientist.com/hottopics/climate/.html

MATERIALS AND THEIR PROPERTIES

Go to: learn.co.uk ▶ Six of the best
▶ Science ▶ KS4 The carbon cycle

⮑ Photosynthesis, digestion and combustion

Do the Carbon Cycle with Captain Carbon on the Chemical Carousel. Suitable for KS2-4.

http://library.thinkquest.org/11226/

⮑ The flow of carbon through the earth's ecosystem

Access this and other excellent Encarta entries on the carbon cycle by keying the above topic into the search box. This material is best suited for KS3-4.

http://encarta.msn.com/encnet/refpages/RefArticle.aspx?refid=761571037&para=20

Go to: learn.co.uk ▶ Six of the best ▶ Science ▶ KS4 Acids and alkalis

➲ The nature of acids and alkalis

A big yes for this colourful site. Don't miss the stuff on the periodic table.

http://www.schoolchem.com/xaa5.htm

Go to: learn.co.uk ▶ Six of the best ▶ Science ▶ KS4 The periodic table

➲ Colourful and impressive interactive periodic table

Be patient – there's a lot to load. Press on an element and the details appear. For greater depth, click 'Chemical data'.

http://www.chemsoc.org/viselements/pages/periodic_table.html

Go to: learn.co.uk ▶ Six of the best
▶ Science ▶ KS4 Kinetic theory

➲ Choose a material and change the temperature

Click an element, set the temperature and watch the molecules jiggle about (or not!).

http://www.miamisci.org/af/sln/phases/

➲ All you need to know if you want to be a solid, liquid or a gas

Fine for KS2-3, especially if you pick a topic and take the full tour.

http://www.chem4kids.com/index.html

➲ Particle arrangement and properties

It asks questions, inspires you to think, and then gives you answers and explanations.

http://www.btinternet.com/~n.j.f/Y7science/
matterweb/particles.htm

➲ Solids, liquids and gases in more detail

Boyle's Law, Kinetic Theory and Gas Laws for KS4.

http://library.thinkquest.org/3659/states/

PHYSICAL PROCESSES

Go to: learn.co.uk ▶ Six of the best ▶ Primary
▶ Materials, forces, the earth and beyond

➲ Royal Observatory, Greenwich

Everything you want to know about cosmology and the universe.

http://www.rog.nmm.ac.uk/leaflets/cosmology/cosmology.html

➲ What is energy?

Hit Energy Quest for fossil fuels to wind power.

http://www.energy.ca.gov/education/story/story-html/story.html

Go to: learn.co.uk ▶ Six of the best
▶ Science ▶ KS4 Electricity

➲ Circuits, charge and resistance

Simple explanations and diagrams of circuits, batteries, electrical charges and resistance.

http://www.cornwallis.kent.sch.uk/intranet/elearn/science/elecmag/1elec_index.html

⊃ Electricity in greater depth

Motion, thermodynamics and heat, modern physics, and electricity.

http://www.physics4kids.com/map.html

Go to: learn.co.uk ▶ Six of the best
▶ Science ▶ KS4 The solar system

⊃ Your weight on other worlds

Good material for KS2-3 – astronomy pictures of the day and views of the solar system – though some of the text is geared to KS4 and beyond. Worth a visit just to find out what you would weigh on Pluto or Mars!

http://www.exploratorium.edu/ronh/weight/

⊃ Journey through the solar system

Brought to you by NASA, who put the first man on the moon. This site is out of this world! 'Star Child' is for 9-12 year-olds and 'Imagine the Universe' is for 13 plus.

http://starchild.gsfc.nasa.gov/docs/StarChild/

Go to: learn.co.uk ▶ Six of the best
▶ Science ▶ KS4 Tectonics

➲ **Movie and quiz covering the basics of continental drift**

Get in the popcorn and watch the Plate Tectonics movie. Pay attention and concentrate – there will be questions later.

http://www.brainpop.com/science/earth/plate tectonics/index.weml

➲ **Interactive features covering the earth's structure, tectonic plates, volcanoes and earthquakes**

Click on KS3 Geography, Earth's Crust for all types of earth-shattering stuff.

http://www.schoolsnet.com/cgi-bin/inetcgi/ schoolsnet/lessons/index.jsp

➲ **Concise account of plate movement and the resulting geological changes**

Serious and detailed stuff for KS4 and beyond.

http://webspinners.com/dlblanc/tectonic/ptbasics.html #plates&boundaries

Go to: learn.co.uk ▶ Six of the best
▶ Science ▶ KS4 Radioactivity

⊃ Radioactivity for KS4 students

Everything you need to know for this topic at
GCSE level.

http://www.darvill.clara.net/nucrad/index.htm

⊃ The nuclear industry

This is the British Nuclear Fuels Limited (BNFL)
site with useful information for all levels.

http://www.bnfl.co.uk/website.nsf/default.htm

GEOGRAPHY

Geography is a subject that has developed enormously, taking in not just the physical environment (e.g. mountains and lakes), but how the environment and related issues (e.g. acid rain, development and tourism) affect people. Because of this, a greater variety and range of resources are needed to solve homework and coursework questions. The following sites are the first gateway to those resources so take note of hyperlinks and recommended links in each site.

Geography teachers advise that reading current newspapers will benefit your understanding and marks. If you've missed a story or want to research a particular topic:

Go to: learn.co.uk ▶ Web guide ▶ History

⊃ The Guardian Century

Here you can search and read original stories that appeared in *The Guardian* newspaper from 1899 to 1999.

http://www.guardiancentury.co.uk/

BRITISH TOWNS AND COUNTRYSIDE

Go to: learn.co.uk ▶ Six of the best ▶ Primary ▶ British towns and countryside

➲ The River Trent

The River Trent is one of only two bore rivers in the UK. Good reference for case studies.

http://www.sln.org.uk/trentweb/

➲ The Peak District national park

KS2-3 homework often involves producing a 'travel' brochure. This site uses the Peak District as an example.

http://www.sln.org.uk/geography/enquiry/we31.htm

➲ Finding your way with map and compass

This detailed site looks at maps and shows you how to read them. Best for KS3 and beyond.

http://mac.usgs.gov/mac/isb/pubs/factsheets/fs03501.html

⊃ Towns of Britain

Quick links to the tourist offices and local councils of large UK towns.

http://www.officialcitysites.org/unitedkingdom.php3

Go to: learn.co.uk ▶ Web guide ▶ Geography

⊃ Essential Guide to Rocks

Includes 10 virtual walks around Britain, tracing the origins of stone and its use in building towns.

http://www.bbc.uk.education/rocks/

⊃ NFU Farm Studies

Nine case studies on various farms in Britain for primary and secondary levels.

http://www.nfu.org.uk/education/farmstud/shtml

⊃ Met Office

All about British weather, including historical weather events.

http://www.met-office.gov.uk/education/

LIMESTONE

Go to: learn.co.uk ▶ Six of the best
▶ Geography ▶ KS3 Limestone

⊃ Types of limestone
A brief morphology (form and structure) of
limestone.
http://www.mineralstech.com/limestone.html

⊃ Malham Cove, Yorkshire
Malham Cove visitor site, but has
good background information on its
landscape and features (e.g. limestone
amphitheatre and pavement).
http://www.yorkshirenet.co.uk/
visinfo/ydales/malham.html

⊃ The Burren, Eire
Five pictures showing the weathered and split
limestone landscape of The Burren.
http://www.geocities.com/TheTropics/Cabana/2973/
Ireland/Burren.html

COASTS

Go to: learn.co.uk ▶ Six of the best
▶ Geography ▶ KS3 Coasts

⮑ **Cliff erosion case study of Beachy Head, East Sussex**

A British Geological Survey of the Beachy Head rockfalls. Loads of resources for KS3.

http://www.bgs.ac.uk/news/events/beachy/beachy.htm

⮑ **Longshore drift**

This site covers landforms and erosion and is a way into the Georesources geography site.

http://www.georesources.co.uk/leld.htm

Go to: learn.co.uk ▶ Six of the best
▶ Geography ▶ KS4 Coast

⮑ **Coasts and human impact in the US**

A detailed site looking at the complex issue of people versus nature.

http://pubs.usgs.gov/circular/c1075/contents.html

RAINFORESTS

> Go to: learn.co.uk ▸ Six of the best
> ▸ Geography ▸ KS3 Rainforest ecosystems

➲ Rainforest map

Maps of rainforests around the world.
http://www.hipark.austin.isd.tenet.edu/projects/fourth
/rainforests/maps/maps.html

➲ Rainforest animals and plants

An overview of rainforest ecology for KS2-3.
http://www.enchantedlearning.com/subjects/
rainforest/

➲ Climate of the forest

A useful KS3 site with
links to other habitats.
http://library.thinkquest.org/
26634/forest/climate.htm

Go to: learn.co.uk ▶ Six of the best
▶ Geography ▶ KS3 Rainforests at risk

➲ People of the rainforest

The Rainforest Foundation supports indigenous rainforest populations in their efforts to protect their environment.

http://www.rainforestfoundationuk.org/rainhome.html

➲ Saving the rainforests

An environmental group explains its case against deforestation. Good background for a case study.

http://www.hipark.austin.isd.tenet.edu/projects/fourth/rainforests/environment.html

➲ Ecotourism simulation

Discover the benefits and drawbacks of tourism in the developing world through an interactive game centred around a family from the Ecadourian Amazon. Very good for KS3 and beyond.

http://www.eduweb.com/ecotourism/eco1.html

See also: Science, pages 55-57.

FLOOD DISASTER

Go to: learn.co.uk ▶ Six of the best
▶ Geography ▶ KS3 Floods

⟳ Types of flood

Easy text explaining floods and causes, prevention
and preparation for KS3-4.
http://library.thinkquest.org/C003603/english/
flooding/causesoffloods.shtml

⟳ The water cycle and storm hydrographs

Compiled for UNESCO's World Day for Water
2000. The information is detailed but clear.
http://www.unesco.org/science/waterday2000/
Cycle.htm

⟳ Coastal flooding

Environment Agency site for KS2-3. Choose your
topics from the pull-down menu.
http://www.environment-agency.gov.uk/education/
schools/stones/stone02.htm

VOLCANOES

Go to: learn.co.uk ▸ Six of the best ▸ Geography ▸ KS3 Volcanoes

⊃ Map of world volcanoes

More than a map with over 60 quick links to active volcano monitoring stations.

http://www.geo.mtu.edu/volcanoes/world.html

⊃ Types of volcano

A chart showing volcano types, shapes, compositions and activities for KS3-4.

http://www.science.ubc.ca/~geol202/igneous/extru/volctypes.html

⊃ Montserrat case study

A huge site which among other things contains daily scientific reports on the volcano.

http://www.geo.mtu.edu/volcanoes/west.indies/soufriere/govt/

See also: Science page 63.

EARTHQUAKES

Go to: learn.co.uk ▶ Six of the best
▶ Geography ▶ KS3 Earthquakes

⊃ Map of tectonic plates

A world map which shows where
earthquakes have occurred over the
past five years, and the relationship
between those quakes and the
tectonic plates.

http://vulcan.wr.usgs.gov/Glossary/PlateTectonics/
Maps/ map_quakes_world_990707_topo.html

⊃ Current earthquakes

Click on an earthquake for the latest information.
http://wwwneic.cr.usgs.gov/neis/current/world.html

⊃ Types of plate boundary

Clear information about divergent, convergent,
transform and plate boundaries.
http://www.cyber.vt.edu/geog1014/TOPICS/
104Disastr/plate/plate.html

ANTARCTICA

Go to: learn.co.uk ▶ Six of the best
▶ Geography ▶ KS3 Antarctic

➲ Wildlife of Antarctica

Though the coldest place on Earth, the seas around Antarctica are teeming with life. Lots of illustrations to print out.

http://www.zoomschool.com/school/Antarctica/Animalprintouts.shtml

➲ Updated webcam of Antarctica

Regularly updated snapshots of everyday happenings at the Macquarie Island Station.

http://www.antdiv.gov.au/stations/macca/video.html

➲ How Antarctica controls world climate

Simple explanations and diagrams, along with experiments.

http://www.geophys.washington.edu/People/Students/ginny/antarctica/lesson3.htm

DESERTS

Go to: learn.co.uk ▶ Six of the best
▶ Geography ▶ KS3 Deserts

➲ Types of desert
Lots of text, but so clearly presented that it is
suitable for all levels. Good links to other
habitat sites.
http://www.ucmp.berkeley.edu/glossary/gloss5/biome/
deserts.html

➲ Plants of the desert
Fascinating look at those plants that survive and
thrive in the desert.
http://mbgnet.mobot.org/sets/desert/tplants.htm

➲ People of the desert, with Kalahari case study
Written by a !Kung Woman, you will discover how
the !Kung tribe survive in the Kalahari.
http://www.ucc.uconn.edu/%7Eepsadm03/kung.html

HISTORY

On the following pages, listed under periods of history or themes, are over 60 sites that will solve homework problems. Here are four general reference sites:

Go to: learn.co.uk ▶ Web guide ▶ History

➲ The British Monarchy
The A-Z of the British monarchy, and Royal art collections and residences.
http://www.royal.gov.uk/

➲ The Guardian Century
Original stories from *The Guardian* – 1899 to 1999.
http://www.guardiancentury.co.uk/

➲ The History of the Millennium
Simply key in the year you want to read about.
http://www.guardian.co.uk/Millennium/0,2833,247428,00.html

➲ History house
An informal look at history for KS4.
http://www.historyhouse.com/

ANCIENT CIVILISATIONS

Go to: learn.co.uk ▶ Six of the best
▶ Primary ▶ Early history

⊃ Ancient Egyptians

Move the cursor over the timeline for a brief
description of each period or search the A-Z.
http://www.ancient-egypt.org/history/

⊃ Ancient Greece

Homework help under the headings of history,
mythology, art, Olympics, wars, the people and
geography. For KS2-4, though KS4 should click
highlighted words for greater detail.
http://www.ancientgreece.com/

⊃ The Romans in Britain

People and events, and cities and daily life in
Roman Britain.
http://www.britainexpress.com/History/
Roman_Britain_index.htm

➲ The Romans

Clear text, pictures, maps and interactive elements.

http://www.roman-empire.net/children

➲ The Celts

Short overview of the Celts – warfare, druids, etc.

http://www.britainexpress.com/History/Celtic_Britain
.htm

> Go to: learn.co.uk ▸ Web guide
> ▸ History ▸ Anglo-saxons

➲ Anglo Saxon England

This site is comprehensive and has some good
primary sources. Best for KS3 and above.

http://emuseum.mankato.msus.edu/prehistory/vikings/
angsaxe.html

> Go to: learn.co.uk ▸ Web guide
> ▸ History ▸ Vikings

➲ The Viking Network Web

Simple text, but click highlighted words for more
information.

http://www.viking.no/e/ewho.htm

WILLIAM THE CONQUEROR

Go to: learn.co.uk ▶ Six of the best ▶ History
▶ William the Conqueror

⟳ Harold II
Biography of the defeated king and
the events of his life.
http://www.britannia.com/history/
monarchs/mon21.html

⟳ William the Conqueror
Biography of the Norman victor.
http://www.britannia.com/history/monarchs/
mon22.html

⟳ The Battle of Hastings
The origins, protagonists, battle plan, and why King
Harold lost.
http://www.bbc.co.uk/history/games/hastings/about/
hastings.shtml

TUDORS

Go to: learn.co.uk ▶ Six of the best ▶ Primary
▶ The Tudors and the Victorians

➲ Who's who in Tudor history

Very good material, especially Henry VIII's music
and Tudor women. All KS levels.

http://home.hiwaay.net/~crispen/tudor/index.html

Go to: learn.co.uk ▶ Six of the best
▶ History ▶ Elizabeth I

➲ The Tudors

Short biographies of the Tudor monarchs aimed
at KS2-3.

http://www.royal.gov.uk/

➲ Elizabethan England

Easy-to-read text on a number of topics suitable
for KS2 upwards.

http://www.springfield.k12.il.us/schools/springfield/
eliz/elizabethanengland.html

➲ Life in Elizabethan England

Over 60 topics – from food to wedding customs
– to add colour to KS3 and beyond projects.
http://www.renaissance.dm.net/compendium/
home.html

➲ Tudor history

Profiles the Tudor dynasty and covers special
topics in Tudor history. For a laugh, go to Tudor
humour and check out The Simpsons' lampooning
of Henry VIII.
http://www.tudorhistory.org/

THE ENGLISH CIVIL WARS

Go to: learn.co.uk ▶ Six of the best
▶ History ▶ The English Civil War

⮑ The Stuarts

Biographies and portraits of the first
Stuart – James I – through to the last.
http://www.royal.gov.uk/

⮑ Oliver Cromwell

Cromwell's life and religion, and the man as a
politician and soldier. Good collection of quotes
by Cromwell and about him, and a plentiful
picture resource.
http://www.cromwell.argonet.co.uk/

⮑ The English civil wars

Good material on the causes and effects, but also
on battle tactics and equipment. Best for KS3-4.
http://easyweb.easynet.co.uk/~crossby/ECW/
index.htm

THE VICTORIANS

Go to: learn.co.uk ▸ Six of the best ▸ Primary
▸ The Tudors and the Victorians

➲ The Victorian period

Biographies, events, Victorian life, culture and art for KS3 onwards.

http://www.britainexpress.com/History/Victorian_index.htm

➲ Lifestyle in Victorian times

Everything about the niceties and etiquette of Victorian life – how to sit, walk, talk and dress.

http://www.victorianstation.com/lifestylemenu.htm

➲ Eminent Victorians

Biographies of Brunel and other Victorians including Disraeli and Charles Dickens. Suitable for KS2 upwards.

http://www.skittler.demon.co.uk/victorians/brunel.htm

THE INDUSTRIAL REVOLUTION

THE RAILWAYS

Go to: learn.co.uk ▶ Six of the best
▶ History ▶ The railways

➲ **Liverpool and Manchester railway**

This is an introduction to the role of the railway in modern industrial society.

http://www.members.axion.net/~igregson/l%26m%20railway/

➲ **George Stephenson**

A short biography with three valuable links.

http://www.britainexpress.com/History/bio/stephenson.htm

➲ **Isambard Kingdom Brunel**

A biography of one of the true pioneers of engineering.

http://sol.brunel.ac.uk/~jarvis/brunelstory/brunel.html

THE FACTORY SYSTEM

Go to: learn.co.uk ▶ Six of the best
▶ History ▶ The factory system

➲ The textile industry

A look at the domestic and factory systems,
inventors and inventions, life in the factory, and
child labour. Good primary resources.

http://www.spartacus.schoolnet.co.uk/Textiles.htm

➲ Women and the industrial revolution

First person accounts by women who worked in
the factories. Best for KS3-4.

http://www.womeninworldhistory.com/lesson7.html

➲ Child labour

The supporters of child labour and
those who fought against it, as well as
conditions in the factories, reforms,
and some frightening statistics.

http://www.spartacus.schoolnet.
co.uk/IRchild.htm

MEDICINE AND PUBLIC HEALTH

Go to: learn.co.uk ▶ Web guide
▶ History ▶ Medicine through time

➲ The Wellcome Trust

'The Wellcome Trust's History of Medicine Gallery' takes a pointed look at needles.
http://webserver1.wellcome.ac.uk/en/old/MlSexhHOMnee.html

➲ Dr John Snow

A stunning site devoted to the work of a 19th century physician and his role in public health. Don't miss the Evolving Map of London.
http://www.ph.ucla.edu/epi/snow.html

➲ Old Operating Theatre, Museum and Herb Garret

Shows operating conditions before anesthetics and antiseptic surgery were introduced.
http://www.thegarret.org.uk/index.htm

SLAVERY

Go to: learn.co.uk ▶ Six of the best
▶ History ▶ Slavery

➲ Slave narratives
Interviewed between 1936-8, 2300 former slaves
from the American South describe their lives.
http://xroads.virginia.edu/~hyper/wpa/wpahome.html

➲ Bristol and slavery
This site covers pre-17th century slavery, why
slaves were traded and plantation life.
http://www.hpslavery.freeservers.com/

➲ Encyclopaedia of slavery
An extremely detailed site about slavery.
http://www.spartacus.schoolnet.co.uk/USAslavery.htm

➲ The terrible transformation
A comprehensive and issue based site that
contains valuable primary resources for KS4.
http://www.pbs.org/wgbh/aia/part1/index.html

WOMEN GET THE VOTE

Go to: learn.co.uk ▶ Six of the best ▶ History ▶ Women and the vote

➲ The emancipation of women: 1750-1920

Leading characters, groups and organisations, along with the strategies and tactics used.

http://www.spartacus.schoolnet.co.uk/women.htm

➲ Women's history

Comprehensive site covering medieval women and women in the workplace, with biographies, sources and women's history encyclopaedia.

http://womenshistory.about.com

➲ Emmeline Pankhurst

A comprehensive look at Emmeline Pankhurst and her methods for gaining the vote.

http://www.lexcie.zetnet.co.uk/emmeline.htm

THE FIRST WORLD WAR

Go to: learn.co.uk ▶ Six of the best
▶ History ▶ The First World War

⮑ Trenches on the web

An enormous site so take a 'Selected Tour' like 'The Soldier's Experience'. A wealth of primary sources, pictures and art. Suitable for KS4.

http://www.worldwar1.com/index.html

⮑ Encyclopaedia of the First World War

Search the topics to find just what you want. Look out for 'Women in the war', statistics and first-hand accounts.

http://www.spartacus.schoolnet.co.uk/FWW.htm

⊃ First World War primary sources archive

Documents – personal, military and government – can be found here, along with photographs and biographies.

http://www.lib.byu.edu/~rdh/wwi

> Go to: learn.co.uk ▸ Online events
> ▸ Treaty of Versailles

⊃ Treaty of Versailles – World War I

Excellent information about all aspects of this historical event. Aimed at KS4.

http://www.learn.co.uk/versailles/contents.htm

THE SECOND WORLD WAR

Go to: learn.co.uk ▶ Six of the best
▶ Primary ▶ The Second World War

➲ The diary of Anne Frank

Here you'll find photos of Anne Frank, the real
diaries, her family's hiding place along with insights
into the character of this remarkable girl.
http://www.annefrank.nl/eng/diary/diary.html

➲ Children of the second world war

The Imperial War Museum site with a KS2 feature
on children in the war. Look here for other
valuable resources.
http://www.iwm.org.uk/education/index.htm

➲ The rise of Adolf Hitler

From birth to dictatorship, as well as WWII and
Holocaust timelines. Best for KS4.
http://www.historyplace.com/worldwar2/riseofhitler/
index.htm

Go to: learn.co.uk ▶ Six of the best
▶ History ▶ Second World War

➲ Grolier history of the second world war

Biographies, photographs and films for KS3-4.

http://gi.grolier.com/wwii/wwii_mainpage.html

➲ Second world war chronology

Significant events from 1918 to November 1946.

http://www.historyplace.com/worldwar2/timeline/ww2time.htm

➲ The Battle of Britain

A vast site that requires careful navigation.

http://www.battleofbritain.net/contents.html

Go to: learn.co.uk ▶ Web guide
▶ History ▶ Second World War

➲ Cybrary of the Holocaust

First-hand accounts and virtual tour of Auschwitz.

http://www.remember.org/

RACE RELATIONS IN THE US

Go to: learn.co.uk ▶ Six of the best ▶ History
▶ Race relations in the US

➲ Martin Luther King
A timeline of the man and the civil rights movement. If you have the plug-in, it is worth listening to King's speeches.
http://seattletimes.nwsource.com/mlk/index.html

➲ Encyclopaedia of the civil rights movement
Here you'll find campaigners (1860-1980) and the turning points, issues, and rights' organisations.
http://www.spartacus.schoolnet.co.uk/USAcivilrights.htm

➲ Civil rights museum
Exhibits with short text, including the Montgomery Bus Boycott and Freedom Rides.
http://www.mecca.org/~crights/cyber.html

DESIGN AND TECHNOLOGY

Here are three great starting points for any design and technology (D&T) project.

Go to: learn.co.uk ▶ Web guide
▶ Design and technology

➲ D & T online
Offers free access to a wide range of D&T materials, resources and software. Topics covered include electronics, packaging, food, environment, pneumatics and manufacturing.
http://www.dtonline.org

➲ Bad Human Factors Designs
Examples of poor design are described and suggestions made for improvements.
http://www.baddesigns.com/examples.html

➲ How stuff works
Detailed and up-to-date information on the workings of a huge range of products and inventions. Suitable for KS2 upwards.
http://www.howstuffworks.com/

MECHANISMS AND STRUCTURES

Go to: learn.co.uk ▶ Six of the best
▶ Primary ▶ Design and technology

➲ How web pages work

The basics of web technology for KS3-4.

http://www.howstuffworks.com/web-page.htm

➲ Mechanisms and structures

Animated images and descriptions of cams, levers, ratchets, etc.

http://www.flying-pig.co.uk/Pages/cam.htm

Go to: learn.co.uk ▶ Six of the best
▶ Design and technology ▶ Folding and
flat pack furniture

➲ Online mechanisms

A learning site covering mechanisms, levers, rotary/linear motors, gears, pulleys and linkages.

http://www.dtonline.org/apps/menu/app.exe?2&6&0

> Go to: learn.co.uk ▶ Six of the best ▶ Design and technology ▶ Personal light source

⮑ Online electronic components information

Resistors, semi-conductors, transducers, switches, capacitors and formulae.

http://www.dtonline.org/apps/infopage/app.exe?3&1&1&0&1&0

> Go to: learn.co.uk ▶ Web guide ▶ Design and technology

⮑ Technology Insight

Compare your project ideas and product development with industry equivalents. An NGFL site so linked directly to the national curriculum.

http://www.technology.org.uk/

PROCESSES AND MATERIALS

Go to: learn.co.uk ▸ Six of the best ▸ Design and technology ▸ Making a metal hand tool

➲ Shaping and forming materials

This link will take you to the homepage, so click Design Technology, then Resistant Materials. Here you'll find lots of relevant topics.

http://www.bbc.co.uk/education/gcsebitesize/design_and_technology/resistant_materials/shaping_processes_rev.shtml

Go to: learn.co.uk ▸ Six of the best ▸ Design and technology ▸ Making an acrylic clock

➲ Using acrylic sheet

Characteristics of the material as well as cleaning, masking, finishing, drilling, forming and joining acrylic.

http://www.actwin.com/fish/diy/acrylic.html

Go to: learn.co.uk ▶ Six of the best
▶ Design and technology ▶ Puzzle in a box

⊃ Thermoplastics and thermosetting plastics

KS4 tutorial about plastic properties and the uses of common thermoplastics. Information is presented in a clear chart.

http://www3.mistral.co.uk/a.davies/CDT10
plasticproperties.htm

Go to: learn.co.uk ▶ Six of the best ▶ Design and technology ▶ Personal light source

⊃ Online manufacturing injection moulding

Technical aspects of injection moulding and equipment.
http://www.dtonline.org/areas/
7/1/index.htm

> Go to: learn.co.uk ▶ Six of the best ▶ Design
> and technology ▶ Making a metal hand tool

⮑ Forging metal

A series of tutorials on how to forge both
functional and decorative items.

http://www.fremlinsforgery.com/tutorials.html

> Go to: learn.co.uk ▶ Six of the best ▶ Design
> and technology ▶ Belt buckles and fasteners

⮑ Foundry metal-casting techniques

Step-by-step photos of foundry metal casting of a
hand-brake drum.

http://www.narrowgauge.iform.com.au/foundry.html

PROJECTS

Go to: learn.co.uk ▶ Web guide
▶ Design and technology

➲ Cool Text
A free online design tool that provides real-time
generation of fonts and logos.
http://www.cooltext.com/

Go to: learn.co.uk ▶ Six of the best
▶ Primary ▶ Design and technology

➲ Making box crafts
Instructions to make dioramas, frames and boxes.
http://www.enchantedlearning.com/crafts

Go to: learn.co.uk ▶ Six of the best ▶ Design
and technology ▶ Making a carrying device

➲ Online folded packages
Folding card to make a zoetrope, for example.
http://www.dtonline.org/areas/7/4/index.htm

⤷ Quirky card projects

Animated models to make, and a catalogue of ideas.

http://www.flying-pig.co.uk/

Go to: learn.co.uk ▸ Six of the best
▸ Design and technology ▸ Folding and
flat pack furniture

⤷ Make your own foldable model dome out of card

Make your own yurt and crystal dome.

http://www.shelter-systems.com/modle.html

Go to: learn.co.uk ▸ Web guide
▸ Design and Technology

⤷ Design Technology Department

Revision topics; quizzes; inventions and inventors; and lighting, furniture and packaging project ideas and information. Best for KS3-4 and above.

http://www.design-technology.org/

➲ Mechanical Toys
Instructions for toys powered by rubber bands, springs, flywheels, candles and gravity.
http://users.bigpond.net.au/mechtoys/

Go to: learn.co.uk ▸ Six of the best
▸ Design and technology ▸ Making a kite

➲ Plans for small kites
Simple instructions for cylinder, Eddy, kimono, batman and bird kites.
http://www.win.tue.nl/~pp/kites/ifosk/plans/plans.html

➲ Kites as educational tools
How to make and fly simple kites.
http://www.gombergkites.com/nkm/index.html

➲ Detailed plans of Cody kites
Detailed plans and instructions to make a fantastic Cody kite. Also, a gallery of other designs, some with plans and specifications.
http://home.sprynet.com/~jmaxworthy/codyplan.htm

RESEARCHING A PROJECT

Go to: learn.co.uk ▶ Six of the best ▶ Design and technology ▶ Making a carrying device

⊃ Packaging information
Industry Council for Packaging and Environment factsheets on environmental topics, history, materials, processes and case studies.
http://www.incpen.org

⊃ Ergonomics
Everything you need to know about ergonomics – the art of making things 'fit' the user.
http://www.ergonomics.org.uk/ergonomics.htm

⊃ Back packs
Catalogue site of back pack designs and specifications.
http://www.bullteksports.com/
catalog/bags.htm

Go to: learn.co.uk ▶ Web guide
▶ Design and Technology

⊃ Resources – melting pot

A link-based site that leads you to a whole world of valuable and quirky D&T resources.
http://www.fortunecity.co.uk/meltingpot/oxford/38/noframes/

Go to: learn.co.uk ▶ Six of the best
▶ Design and technology ▶ Puzzle in a box

⊃ Game and game companies

A great place to research for ideas.
http://www.dealtime.com/dealtime2000/Pages/Category/0,2469,989-137-1,00.html??bNewUser=0

Go to: learn.co.uk ▶ Six of the best ▶ Design
and technology ▶ Making an acrylic clock

➲ A history of time-keeping and clocks

A walk through time covering history,
development of modern time-keeping machines
and a photo gallery of examples.
http://physics.nist.gov/GenInt/Time/early.html

➲ Children's plastic motion clocks

Some really wonderful, wacky creations.
http://www.infoperson.com/w001n001.htm

Go to: learn.co.uk ▶ Six of the best
▶ Design and technology ▶ Making a kite

➲ How to build a Cody kite

Historical photos, original plans and
a brief history of the Cody kite.
http://www.cody-kites.co.uk/

> Go to: learn.co.uk ▶ Six of the best ▶ Design
> and technology ▶ Making a metal hand tool

➲ **Metal working resources page**

Over 100 links to educational resources and
examples of work.

http://www.makersgallery.com/goss/Links.html

> Go to: learn.co.uk ▶ Six of the best ▶ Design
> and technology ▶ Belt buckles and fasteners

➲ **Examples of cast buckles and
fasteners**

Fasteners for shoes, apparel, industry,
leather goods, headwear and machinery.

http://www.sxindustries.com/

➲ **Custom-made metal-cast buckles**

A catalogue of ideas for buckles, key chains, letter
openers, medallions and tiepins.

http://www.tortolani.com/beltbuckles.html

FOOD TECHNOLOGY

(See also Science, page 54)

Go to: learn.co.uk ▶ Web guide
▶ Design and Technology

➲ Foodlink, Foodfitness, Foodfuture

Three sites for the price of one covering food safety (Foodlink), healthy eating (Foodfitness) and the GM debate (Foodfuture).
http://www.foodlink.org.uk/ http://www.foodfitness.org.uk/ http://www.foodfuture.org.uk/

➲ Food Technology

All aspects of FT for KS4, including food science, processes, and product development.
http://www.foodtech.org.uk/

➲ British Nutrition Foundation

Food technology activities across all the key stages, as well as nutritional facts and information.
http://www.nutrition.org.uk/

➲ British Meat Foundation

Recipes, health, news and loads of
links for everything meaty.
http://www.meatmatters.com/

➲ Vegetarian Society

Link located within the British Meat Foundation
entry. Loads of help for GCSE projects.
http://www.vegsoc.org/

➲ All about eggs

Recipes, nutritional information and egg-citing things!
http://www.eggsedu.org.uk/

➲ The Milk Education Zone

A comprehensive guide to dairy products and
their origin. Good for KS3.
http://www.milk.org.uk/

➲ Seafish Education Site

Hit 'Schools' on homepage for homework help.
http://www.seafish.co.uk/education/

⮑ Institute of Food Science and Technology

This site is run by the professional organisation of food scientists. There are some gems of research and news for coursework. Go to 'School science and food' for foodie experiments on enzymes and chemical raising agents, for example, and links. Best for KS4.

http://www.ifst.org/

⮑ British Nutrition Foundation

Some sound material here for primary and secondary, and also for food and health as part of general science and PSHE. There are career profiles and KS4 exam help. The home page features some interesting articles that may help KS3-4.

http://www.nutrition.org.uk/

ART, DRAMA AND MUSIC

ART

Whether you're doing fine art, graphics, art and design or textiles, you'll find homework and coursework help on these sites and their links.

Go to: learn.co.uk ▶ Six of the best ▶ Primary ▶ The Arts

➲ Art gallery for children

Examples of kids' paintings from around the world (some terrific ideas) and links to art education.

http://www.theartgallery.com.au/kidsart.html

Go to: learn.co.uk ▶ Web guide ▶ Art

➲ Virtual art gallery

Read the story while it takes you on a tour of a virtual art gallery. Best for KS2.

http://www.Eduweb.com/insideart/index.html

➲ Hands-on art

Make 3D models, create some art, design a house and visit Leonardo da Vinci's workshop. There's also a useful glossary and a timeline.

http://www.sanford-artedventures.com/play/play.html

➲ Colorcube

Colorcube is an educational 'toy' for teaching colour theory. The site includes vibrant downloadable images and articles about colour, digital colour and mixing colours. KS3 and beyond.

http://www.colorcube.com/index.htm

➲ Great Buildings

Head here for stunning 3D models and ideas.

http://www.greatbuildings.com/

➲ Eyes on Art

Encourages you to look at paintings and understand 'visual language'. For information about art history periods/movements, click on 'No Fear O'Eras'. Good for KS3-4.

http://www.kn.pacbell.com/wired/art2/index.html

⊃ New York graffiti

Discover the work of Keith Haring, a New York graffiti artist who died in 1988.
http://www.Haringkids.com/

⊃ Art History Resources on the Web

A huge link-based site taking in all art history periods/movements and major artists. Through the museum link you can do a virtual tour of art galleries around the world. KS3 and beyond, though some linked sites are very academic.
http://witcombe.sbc.edu/ARTHLinks.html

Go to: learn.co.uk ▶ Web guide
▶ Art ▶ Gallery

⊃ The Tate Gallery

Go online to all the Tate museums and access the collection of 50,000 images, most with background text.
http://www.tate.org.uk/home/default.htm

DRAMA

In addition to the sites here, drama students should also check out the English drama sites recommended on pages 21-23.

> Go to: learn.co.uk ▶ Six of the best
> ▶ Primary ▶ The Arts

➲ Shakespeare's Globe theatre
Archaeology of the Globe theatre.
http://www.rdg.ac.uk./globe/

➲ Greek drama
Short text covering origins, ancient stagecraft and influences on later drama for KS3 and above.
http://didaskalia.berkeley.edu/Didintro.html

> Go to: learn.co.uk ▶ Web guide
> ▶ English ▶ Drama

⊃ Drama ideas

Plays suitable for various levels and among other articles, there's one on Ancient Greek masks.

http://www.geocities.com/Broadway/Alley/3765/lessons.html/

⊃ The Costume Page

Packed with presentation ideas for anyone putting on a play. An illustrated history of costume will be useful for both drama and textile design.

http://members.aol.com/nebula5/costume.html

⊃ Creative Drama

Your teachers will love this site, so keep one step ahead of their class plans by checking out theatre games and plays.

http://www.creativedrama.com/

⊃ V&A theatre museum

Britain's National Museum of the Performing Arts contains the key collections on the British stage and online video archives of stage performances.

http://theatremuseum.vam.ac.uk/eduindex.htm

MUSIC

These five sites just about cover the music curriculum. There are reference sites for projects, and budding composers and performers should head to 'The Music Land' for composition, theory and aural tests.

> Go to: learn.co.uk ▶ Six of the best
> ▶ Primary ▶ The Arts

➲ Instruments of the orchestra
A site that will wake you up! Listen to the instruments of the orchestra while reading about them. Also read up on sound as energy. Suitable for all levels.
http://tqjunior.thinkquest.org/5116

➲ The great composers
Click on a composer (there are sixteen, including Bach and Vivaldi), listen to the music, and read the biographies. Suitable for all levels.
http://www.geocities.com/Vienna/Strasse/1498/

➲ The electric guitar

Click on 'Home' for the Smithsonian Institute. Hit 'Where to find' and then scroll the A-Z for 'Music and Musical Instruments'. Here you'll find information on the rise of the electric guitar, lots of other instruments as well as performances.
http://www.si.edu/

➲ Encyclopedia of percussion

Alphabetical description and photographs of percussion instruments from around the world.
http://www.cse.ogi.edu/Drum/encyclopedia/

➲ The music land

You must register before you get to the good stuff like online aural and theory tests, and articles and resources. The site is divided into sections for KS3, KS4 and A-level.
http://www.themusicland.co.uk

MODERN LANGUAGES

The selection of foreign language sites recommended on pages 124-141 is just the tip of the iceberg. There are hundreds more to be discovered on **learn.co.uk Six of the best**, the **Web guide** and **Guardian resources**. New sites are regularly added and even more of the modern languages curriculum is being covered. Homework help for Welsh and classical languages is found in the **Web guide**.

FRENCH

If you need to go over a topic in order to make sense of homework or coursework, go to learn.co.uk > **Online lessons and tests**, and then to the French lesson for your year group (years 7, 8 and 9 in KS3) or for KS4. These lessons cover the curriculum and will take you through every aspect of language and themes.

Go to: learn.co.uk ▸ Web guide ▸ Modern languages ▸ French

⮑ **Really Useful French Teaching Site**

Presented in French and English, this site knows exactly what you need for homework assignments and gives it to you. Aimed at KS4.

http://www.btinternet.com/~s.glover/S.Glover/ languagesite/Default.htm

⮑ **About French**

An educational site with features on grammar and quizzes. There are 1400 sound labs. Aimed at beginners, intermediate and advanced students.

http://french.about.com/mbody.htm

➲ French for all at all levels

This website contains everything you need to revise for French at all levels. There are interactive exercises for listening, speaking, reading and writing.
http://web.ukonline.co.uk/canonave/

➲ Voici la France

Resources for history, geography, economy and political climate of France. Advanced students can read the original texts; other levels can read the English translation.
http://www.france.diplomatie.fr/Thema/dossier.asp?
DOS=DECOUVRIR

➲ Funambule

Watch the TV5 video clips, then do the comprehension questions. For each clip, there is usually an associated section giving cultural background or similar. Suitable for KS3 onwards.
http://www.funambule.com/cgi-bin/tv5.asp

➲ Le Monde

The most prestigious French daily newspaper.
http://www.lemonde.fr/

FRENCH TOPICS FOR KS4

Though these are special topics of interest for KS4 French, there are sites here that will also help with KS3 homework.

> Go to: learn.co.uk ▶ Six of the best
> ▶ French ▶ Je me présente

➲ Horoscope for the day

A magazine-style site in French with teen pages, jobs, leisure, news, health and horoscopes.

http://www.lokace.com

> Go to: learn.co.uk ▶ Six of the best
> ▶ French ▶ La vie scolaire

➲ Up-to-the-minute site on a school specialising in fashion

All about a school in Paris – Le Lycée de la Mode – that specialises in fashion design for those wanting a career in couture ateliers.

http://www.lycee-mode.com

➲ French school life

Everything you might want to know for a project. There's also revision material on core subjects in French.

http://www.orientation.fr/lycee.htm

> Go to: learn.co.uk ▸ Six of the best
> ▸ French ▸ Les divertissements

➲ Books, BDs, games and stories ...

Here you'll find latest cinema blockbusters, book reviews, music features and school information. There's also a dictionary and reference section.

http://www.momes.net/

> Go to: learn.co.uk ▸ Web guide
> ▸ Modern languages ▸ French

➲ The World Cup

A good starting point for football fans doing an assignment on leisure and hobbies.

http://www.worldcup.fr/

Go to: learn.co.uk ▶ Six of the best
▶ French ▶ Les professions

⊃ Improve your self-knowledge

Hand-writing analysis, personality and leadership tests, and interview techniques.

http://www.chez.com/recrutement

⊃ How would you fare at interview?

Thirty questions to help you work out what sort of job you would like and your attitude to a career.

http://www.telema.fr/TRAV31

⊃ Find your ideal job

Job vacancies in marketing, technology, industry, finance and health, etc.

http://www.ifrance.com/heberg

Go to: learn.co.uk ▶ Six of the best
▶ French ▶ Visite à Paris

➲ A virtual tour of the Centre Pompidou in Paris

Current and upcoming exhibitions, collections and education/research sites.

http://www.centrepompidou.fr

➲ Find the right museum in France

From here you can find details of galleries all over France, although the yellow type can be a little hard to read.

http://www.artiste.free.fr

➲ Choose the ideal hotel at Versailles

Find somewhere to stay and organise a tour.

http://www.mairie-versailles.fr

Go to: learn.co.uk ▶ Six of the best
▶ French ▶ Les magasins

⊃ Services and products from the biggest sports chain in France

A catalogue of Supersport gear.

http://www.supersport.fr

⊃ The famous Printemps store

Shop till you virtually drop in this gorgeous store.

http://www.printemps.fr

⊃ Lively shopping centre with animations

Take a tour around the 80 shops
in Saint Clair mall.

http://www.centresaint-clair.com

Go to: learn.co.uk ▶ Six of the best
▶ French ▶ La santé (Healthy lifestyle)

⊃ Recipe suggestions for healthy eating

The homepage for the French magazine *Elle* with its sections on design, food, health, beauty and fashion.

http://www.elle.fr

⊃ Alternative to healthy living, with the Simpsons

The official site for 'The Simpsons' with profiles of all the characters and video clips of each episode. Very funny!

http://www.multimania.com/simpsons

GERMAN

Following are sites that will help KS2-KS4 with German topic work – food, travel, hobbies and leisure, youth culture, etc. On page 136 you'll find help for grammar and language questions.

Go to: learn.co.uk ▶ Web guide
▶ Modern languages ▶ German

➲ Butterbrot

Everything you want to know about the German open sandwich. Construct your favourite sandwich and brush up on food vocabulary.
http://www.butterbrot.de/index.html

➲ Schulweb

The homepages of schools throughout Germany, presented region by region. Each site may include a school magazine, local news and topical issues. Aimed at KS4.
http://www.schulweb.de/

➲ At the department store
Go on a virtual German shopping trip at Karstadt.
http://www.karstadt.de/webapp/commerce/servlet/
CategoryDisplay?merchant_rn=2745&cgrfnbr=17845

➲ Freizeittip
A great resource for holiday and lifestyle modules.
Click on a sport and find out what's on.
http://www.freizeittip.de/

➲ Borussia
Read up on Borussia-Dortmund in Deustch.
http://www.borussia-dortmund.de/

➲ Christmas celebrations
Head here for comprehension, vocabulary or for
a cultural question on the Christmas tradition.
http://www.weihnachtsseite.de/

➲ Naturschutzorganisation WWF
The German site of the World Wild Fund for
Nature is wide-ranging so is a good resource for
'My World' and 'The Young Person in Society' topics.
http://www.wwf.de/

⊃ Jetzt

This site offers reading strategies and practice. There is an extensive set of texts that are linked to an excellent glossary with usage examples and grammar support.

http://www.goethe.de/z/jetzt/

⊃ Juma

A German language magazine for English teenagers.

http://www.juma.de/

⊃ Germany online

An excellent German Embassy site with headlines from Germany, online audio from 'Germany Today' and film clips.

http://www.germany-info.org/f_index.html

➲ Eine Reise durch Deutschland

An Australian primary
school site that covers
the German language and
cultural topics. Also a
collection of German
fairytales of varying
difficulty for reading or
comprehension with English
translations. Perfect for KS2-KS4.

http://www.bayswaterps.vic.edu.au/lote/BLOTE.htm

➲ Really Useful German Site

This site was designed by a teacher who knows
exactly what resources and homework help you
need. Games, downloads, quizzes, seasonal
themes, a photo gallery, and more for KS4 level.
http://atschool.eduweb.co.uk/haberg/reallyusefulge/
default.htm

➲ Die Zeit

A quality German daily newspaper.
http://www3.zeit.de/zeit/

➲ Handbook of grammar

This site is being constantly updated, but at present it offers basic, essential grammar. Well worth a visit.

http://www.travlang.com/languages/german/ihgg/

➲ The German Electronic Textbook

Grammar, pronunciation (download to hear the sounds as they should be said) and vocabulary.

http://www.wm.edu/CAS/modlang/grammnu.html

➲ German-English dictionary

A general English/German dictionary.

http://dict.tu-chemnitz.de/

➲ Quickdic

A downloadable dictionary with 170,000 entries.

http://www.quickdic. de/index_e.html

SPANISH

Check out **On the web** at **learn.co.uk** > **Guardian resources** > **Secondary** for more website help with Español homework.

> Go to: learn.co.uk ▶ Web guide
> ▶ Modern Languages ▶ Spanish

⇒ BBC Education
For all levels, from beginner to advanced, there are grammar basics, listening and speaking exercises, video clips and audio conversations, and games.
http://www.bbc.co.uk/education/languages/spanish/index.shtml

⇒ Learn Spanish
Basic vocabulary listed under topics like Christmas, football, music, professions, shops, personality and appearance. All lists are printable and useful for any level.
http://www.lingolex.com/spanish.htm

➲ Learn Spanish –
A Free Online Tutorial

Eighty-four grammar lessons from the gender of nouns to subjunctives. Though the topics become advanced, the same clear explanation style is used. Very good for beginners upwards.

http://www.studyspanish.com/tutorial.htm

➲ Instituto Cervantes

A language-learning site that also provides cultural information, news and activities for beginners through to advanced Spanish speakers. Extracts from novels have hyperlinks to aid comprehension and vocabulary.

http://cvc.cervantes.es/portada.htm

➲ Si, Spain

A magazine-style site that gives information on geography, society, economy and trade, education, tourism and customs. This site can be read in Spanish or English.

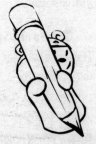

http://www.sispain.org/

➲ El País
A Spanish national newspaper.
http://www.elpais.es/

➲ Diccionario Anaya
You can translate English to Spanish or vice-versa. Easy to use and the results of your search appear quickly and they are comprehensive. Best for KS4 and above, but so simple to use KS3 will also benefit.
http://www.diccionarios.com/

➲ Activa
A Spanish-English technical and business dictionary for downloading.
http://www.activadic.com/

WORLD LANGUAGES

Sites that cover many languages, often include less common languages (in other words, not English, French, German or Spanish) or provide translation services.

Go to: learn.co.uk ▶ Web guide
▶ Modern languages

➲ Sounds of the World's Animals
Discover how the Dutch would make the 'hee-haw' of a donkey or how a Chinese monkey sounds.
http://www.georgetown.edu/cball/animals/animals.html

➲ Less Commonly-Taught Languages
There is a useful picture album, audio-video archives and an 'Ask the Expert' service for languages from Basque and Chinese to Polish and Portugese.
http://carla.acad.umn.edu/lctl/lctl.html

⊃ Translation resource

Games and learning, tests and quizzes, culture and language (including origin, vocabulary, forms of address, grammar and survival phrases) for languages from Arabic to Ukrainian. Also a translation service for emails and documents.
http://www.transparent.com/languagepages/languages.htm

Go to: learn.co.uk ▸ Web guide ▸ Modern Languages ▸ German

⊃ German Online

Not just German, but also Albanian, Chinese, Croatian, French, Italian, Latin, Portuguese, Russian and Spanish language lessons, covering reading, listening, speaking, pronunciation and grammar. There are also quizzes and cultural topics.
http://eleaston.com/german.html

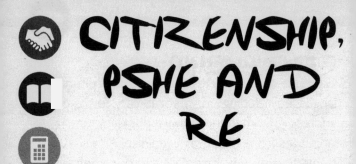

CITIZENSHIP, PSHE AND RE

CITIZENSHIP

The sites listed in this section relate to the schemes of work for KS3-4, including human rights, cooperation, conflict and tolerance, democracy and autocracy, and sustainable development. For resources on other KS3-4 topics – community involvement, global citizenship, central and local government, the legal system, money and finance, and media in society – go to **Six of the best** and then click on 'Citizenship'. There are also sites suitable for KS2 here as well.

HUMAN RIGHTS

Go to: learn.co.uk ▸ Six of the best ▸
Citizenship ▸ Human rights

➲ Amnesty International
Latest news on AI campaigns on injustices around the world, and a look back at Amnesty's contribution and quotes from those it has helped.
http://www.amnesty.org.uk

➲ Black and white slavery today

This site is run by Anti-Slavery International.
You'll find their campaigns and current reports
on slavery worldwide.
http://www.antislavery.org

➲ The Commission for Racial Equality

Head for the site map where you'll find features
on immigrants past and present, contributions of
ethnic minorities, employment practices, and
opportunities in education, housing, and sport.
http://www.cre.gov.uk/

➲ UNICEF

Click 'Education' for campaigns
and issues related to the UN
Convention on the Rights of
the Child. 'Voice of Youth' is a
special section with discussion
rooms, activities and problems
to solve. For news stories go to
'News'. Suitable for all levels.
http://www.unicef.org.uk

➲ Up-to-the-minute reports on human rights issues

Though heavily aimed at teachers, the 'Global Express' link provides alternative world news sources and current stories. For project material, click for a free sample of the *Global Express* magazine.

http://www.dep.org.uk/globalexpress/

COOPERATION, CONFLICT AND TOLERANCE

Go to: learn.co.uk ▶ Six of the best ▶ Citizenship ▶ Cooperation, conflict and tolerance

➲ Conflict resolution

How to set up a school council and the benefits of a charter of behaviour. There is also a section on encouraging tolerance and building resolution skills in the playground.

http://www.schoolcouncils.org/

◓ World conflict and cooperation

Everything you need to know about the United Nations and its member states around the world. Click on 'Cyber School Bus' for profiles of the member states – population, area, economic statistics, for example – and current issues.
http://www.un.org/

◓ Site linking students in areas that do not have racial diversity

Britkid's site is about race, racism and life as seen through the eyes of the Britkid characters. Once registered, play the games, do the quizzes and reveal all (or nothing!) in 'Truth and Dare'. In 'Serious Issues' you'll find UK language and religious groups, immigration law, terminology about race, 'Stop and Search' laws, sport and racism, and useful maps.
http://www.britkid.org/

DEMOCRACY AND AUTOCRACY

Go to: learn.co.uk ▶ Six of the best ▶
Citizenship ▶ Democracy and autocracy

➲ How parliament works

The Act of Parliament and special features which
will open the door of the Palace of Westminster
for you. For KS2 level material, click on 'Junior'.
http://www.explore.parliament.uk/

➲ Political and legal issues for
young people

The Citizenship Foundation site has the latest
news on issues like asylum and the Human Rights
Act. There are also features and links to the
'United Kingdom Youth Parliament' and 'Children's
Express' (a project to help 8-18 year-olds learn
through journalism). Click on 'Schoolzone' for
homework and revision help, Internet projects
and resources, and tips to handle stress.
http://www.citfou.org.uk

SUSTAINABLE DEVELOPMENT

Go to: learn.co.uk ▶ Six of the best ▶
Citizenship ▶ Sustainable development

⊃ Development ideas for young people
Global Eye magazine looks at world development
issues in food production.
http://www.globaleye.org.uk

⊃ Friends of the Earth
FOE's current campaigns include world trade, real
food, safer chemicals and climate talks.
http://www.foe.co.uk/

Go to: learn.co.uk ▶ Web guide ▶ Citizenship

⊃ Imagine London
Your ideas for improving London.
http://www.imaginelondon.org.uk/

⊃ The Development Education Project
A major feature on the sustainable environment.
http://www.dep.org.uk/

PSHE

PERSONAL, SOCIAL, HEALTH EDUCATION

In addition to the topics covered here, the PSHE section on the **learn.co.uk Web guide** also includes: drug and substance abuse, alcohol abuse, smoking, crime and crime prevention, money and finance, environmental issues and ethics (abortion and euthanasia).

Go to: learn.co.uk ▶ Web guide ▶ PSHE

➲ Health Education Board for Scotland
Check out the home page features, then click 'Specialist Sites' to get into the 'Cyberschool' where you can search the index for a special topic. 'O2' has topics like modelling for teenagers, while 'Classroom' deals with the essentials of drugs, alcohol, diet and smoking. Quizzes and games are in the 'Common Room'. Suitable for KS2 and above.
http://www.hebs.org.uk/

➲ Health Education

Click on Movie and take your pick from over 50 health movies – acne to voice!

http://www.brainpop.com

➲ Mind, Body and Soul

A great site with good links if you need information on accidents, alcohol, drugs, healthy eating, mental health, physical activity, sex health, smoking and sun protection. Best for KS4.

http://www.mindbodysoul.gov.uk/

Go to: learn.co.uk ▸ Web guide ▸ PSHE ▸ Childbirth & parenting

➲ Childbirth.org

A magazine-style site where you can read current features or search the archives for a particular topic. The information is geared to parents-to-be.

http://www.childbirth.org/

⊃ All About Kids

A directory of parenting sites, but the home page does highlight some interesting features. For example, children who are overweight, talking about death and sorting behavioural problems.
http://www.aak.com/

Go to: learn.co.uk ▶ Web guide
▶ PSHE ▶ Relationships

⊃ The History of Marriage

A history of marriage and the forms it can take in different cultures. Best suited to KS4 and above.
http://marriage.miningco.com/library/weekly/aa070198.htm

Go to: learn.co.uk ▶ Web guide
▶ PSHE ▶ Sex education

⊃ Lovelife

The Health Education Authority's sexual health website. Articles on resisting the pressure to have sex, safer sex and contraception.
http://www.lovelife.uk.com

⊃ Sex Education, Sex and Aids

A really good site that talks to you in a straight-forward manner. Check out the FAQs or look at relationships and feelings, sex for the first time, contraception, and issues like the age of consent.
http://www.avert.org/sexnaids.htm

Go to: learn.co.uk ▶ Web guide
▶ PSHE ▶ Society

⊃ Action Aid

This organisation's vision is 'a world without poverty in which every person can experience their right to life with dignity'. This site is definitely worth checking out.
http://www.actionaid.org

⊃ CARE

Cooperative for Assistance and Relief Everywhere is an international charity working in places like Bolivia and Madagascar. The information centre has news reports and photo and video galleries.
http://www.care.org/

⮑ Poverty Net

A World Bank site – huge but easy to search – that is a great place to learn about poverty and inequality and how both can be alleviated. Don't miss 'Voices of the Poor'.

http://www.worldbank.org/poverty/

⮑ United Nations High Commission for Refugees

Comprehensive information about the work of the UNHCR which currently cares for 22 million people. A heart-breaking picture gallery.

http://www.unhcr.ch/cgi-bin/texis/vtx/home

⮑ War On Want

Information on current campaigns against poverty in places like Colombia and Western Sahara, and the group's progress and position on debt relief and fair trade. The site calls for your support and involvement.

http://www.waronwant.org/

RELIGIOUS EDUCATION

In addition to these recommended sites for KS3 and above, these faiths are listed separately under 'Religion' on the **Web guide**: Anglicanism, Buddhism, Catholicism, Protestantism, Hinduism, Islam, Judaism, Sikhism and Christianity.

KS2 students should go to: **Guardian resources > Primary > On the web** to discover other world religion sites to help with RE homework.

Go to: learn.co.uk ▶ Guardian resources ▶ Primary ▶ On the web ▶ World religions

➲ **RE resources**
Click on the pull-down menu for the faith and age level (KS1 upwards) or specify a topic. The site clearly lists hyperlinks on the faith or topic.
http://www.allre.org.uk/allre/index.html

⊃ GCSE Religious Studies revision

This KS4 site covers Buddhism, Christianity, Islam, Judaism and Roman Catholicism, perspectives topics and Mark's Gospel. There is also a handy glossary, links provided at the end of each topic and good revision exercises. Over 1,317 UK secondary schools use this site. Excellent, well-organised and comprehensive.

http://re-xs.ucsm.ac.uk/gcsere/index.html

⊃ Religious Movements

An easy to navigate site that has detailed profiles of over 200 religious movements from Adidam to Zoroastrianism via Buddhism, Islam, and Quaker. Articles are quite long, but fascinating reading for KS4 and beyond.

http://religiousmovements.lib.virginia.edu/profiles/profiles.htm

➲ Religious tolerance

Essays on many religions and ethical systems
written by authors of different faiths whose
genuine aim is the promotion of religious
tolerance. Valuable for KS4 and above.

http://www.religioustolerance.org/

➲ The Interfaith calendar

Simply click on the year and the calendar pops up.
Go to the 'A-Z Definition of Terms' to have feasts
and festivals explained or to 'Families of Religions'
for descriptions. Suitable for all levels.

http://www.interfaithcalendar.org/

I t can take a little bit of time to become totally confident researching on the Internet. But 'Where am I now?' questions are soon replaced by 'Where can I go to now?'. The information available seems infinite and with one click, a hyperlink can take you anywhere, everywhere, and sometimes nowhere! Write down what you need to get from your Internet search and stick to it!

With so much out there, web surfers often wonder if they are on the best site. This Internet version of 'the grass is always greener some-where else' syndrome shouldn't worry you if you stick to the highly recommended sites in this book and the hundreds of others on **learn.co.uk**

Once you've found the material you need, it is easy (and so much fun!) to keep surfing. But there comes a time when you have to sign off and start turning words off the web into words of your own. A huge pile of print-outs will bulk out your homework, but the real gain is transforming downloads into notes you understand. Go to it!

WANT TO KNOW MORE?

Look out for these other titles developed in association with **learn.co.uk**

Revision Sorted! by Kate Brookes
Life saving revision tips in a handy format. Every student at some point has to face up to the ghastly reality of EXAMS. This book staves off panic and confusion with its calm and practical advice, on everything from revision plans and methods to stress-busting strategies and top exam techniques. All presented in easily digestible chunks and a reassuring style – SORTED!

Homework Sorted! by Kate Brookes

An essential pocket-sized guide to better homework. *Homework Sorted!* shows you how to get organised – deciding where and when to work, getting the right equipment and planning study time effectively. It's also packed with time-saving advice on finding the information you need, including useful organisations and websites recommended by **learn.co.uk**. All presented in easily digestible chunks and a reassuring style – SORTED!

Other titles by Hodder Children's Books

the txt book by Kate Brookes

The best text message book ever! All the abbreviations, acronyms and similes you will ever need, together with lots of hints on expert texting. Packed with essential messages for all aspects of life, together with a few to make you giggle...

Little Book of Exam Skills by Kate Brookes
Prepare yourself for exams with this little book. It's packed with brilliant revision tips you can start using *right now* – plus top exam techniques to help you make the grade!

Little Book of Exam Calm by Anita Naik
Keep your cool at exam time with the help of this little book. Packed with advice on how to stay happy and healthy before and during your exams, it will provide you with a calm and confident route to exam success!

You can buy all these books from your local bookseller, or order them direct from the publisher. For more information, write to:

The Sales Department, Hodder Wayland, a division of Hodder Headline Limited, 338 Euston Road, London, NW1 3BH.

Visit our website at:
www.madaboutbooks.com